GARDEN FRESH
Vegetables

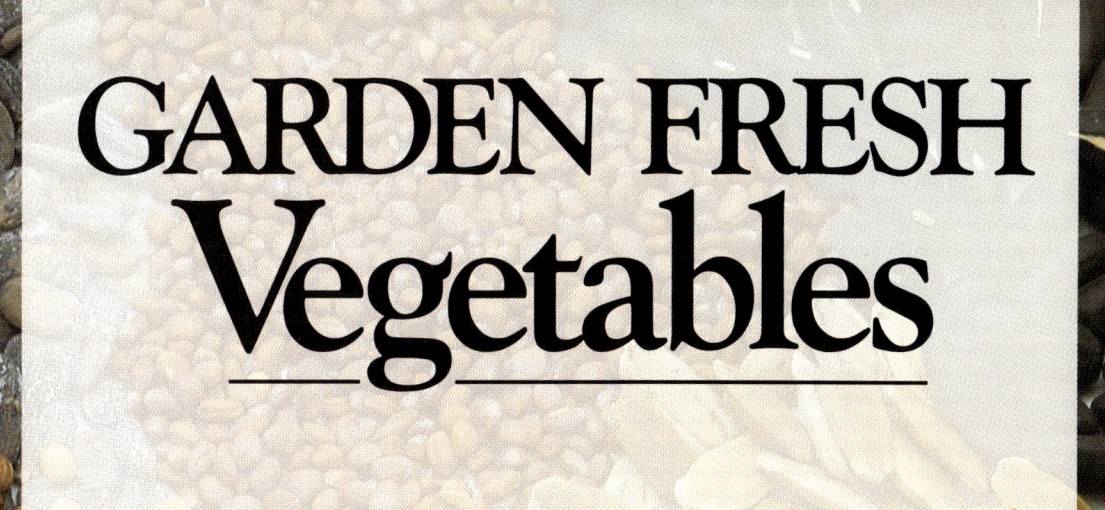

WRITER
BOB DOLEZAL

PHOTOGRAPHER
ALAN COPELAND

ILLUSTRATOR
BUNNY CARTER

AVON BOOKS ◆ NEW YORK

If you purchased this book without a cover, you should be aware that this book is stolen property. It was reported as "unsold and destroyed" to the publisher, and neither the author nor the publisher has received any payment for this "stripped book."

Acquisition, Development and Production Services by BMR, of Corte Madera, CA

Acquisition: JACK JENNINGS, BOB DOLEZAL

Series Concept: BOB DOLEZAL

Developmental Editing: BOB DOLEZAL

Photographic Director: ALAN COPELAND

Cover Photo: ALAN COPELAND

Interior Art: BUNNY CARTER

North American Map: RON HILDEBRAND

Copy Editing: NAOMI LUCKS, JANET REED

Proofreader: TOM HASSETT

Typography and Page Layout: BARBARA GELFAND

Index: SYLVIA COATES

Horticulturist and Site Scout: PEGGY HENRY

Color Separations: PREPRESS ASSEMBLY INCORPORATED

Printing and Binding: PENDELL PRINTING INC.

Production Management: THOMAS E. DORSANEO, JANE RYAN

Film: FUJI VELVIA

Special thanks to Mudd's Restaurant, San Ramon, CA; Alex and Filomena Salada, Sonoma, CA; and Bill Fuijimoto, Monterey Market, CA

91   92   93   94   95   10   9   8   7   6   5   4   3   2   1

GARDEN FRESH VEGETABLES Copyright © 1991 by NK Lawn and Garden Co. All rights reserved. Printed in the United States of America. No part of this book may be used or reproduced in any manner whatsoever without written permission except in the case of brief quotations embodied in critical articles and reviews. For information address BMR, 21 Tamal Vista Blvd., Suite 209, Corte Madera, CA 94925.

First Avon Books Trade Printing: February 1992

ISBN: 0-380-76662-0

Library of Congress Catalog Card Number: 91-67352

Notice: The information contained in this book is true and complete to the best of our knowledge. All recommendations are made without any guarantees on the part of the authors, NK Lawn and Garden Co., or BMR. Because the means, materials and procedures followed by homeowners are beyond our control, the author and publisher disclaim all liability in connection with the use of this information.

AVON BOOKS
A division of
The Hearst Corporation
1350 Avenue of the Americas
New York, New York 10019

AVON TRADEMARK REG. U.S. PAT. OFF.
AND IN OTHER COUNTRIES, MARCA
REGISTRADA, HECHO EN U.S.A.

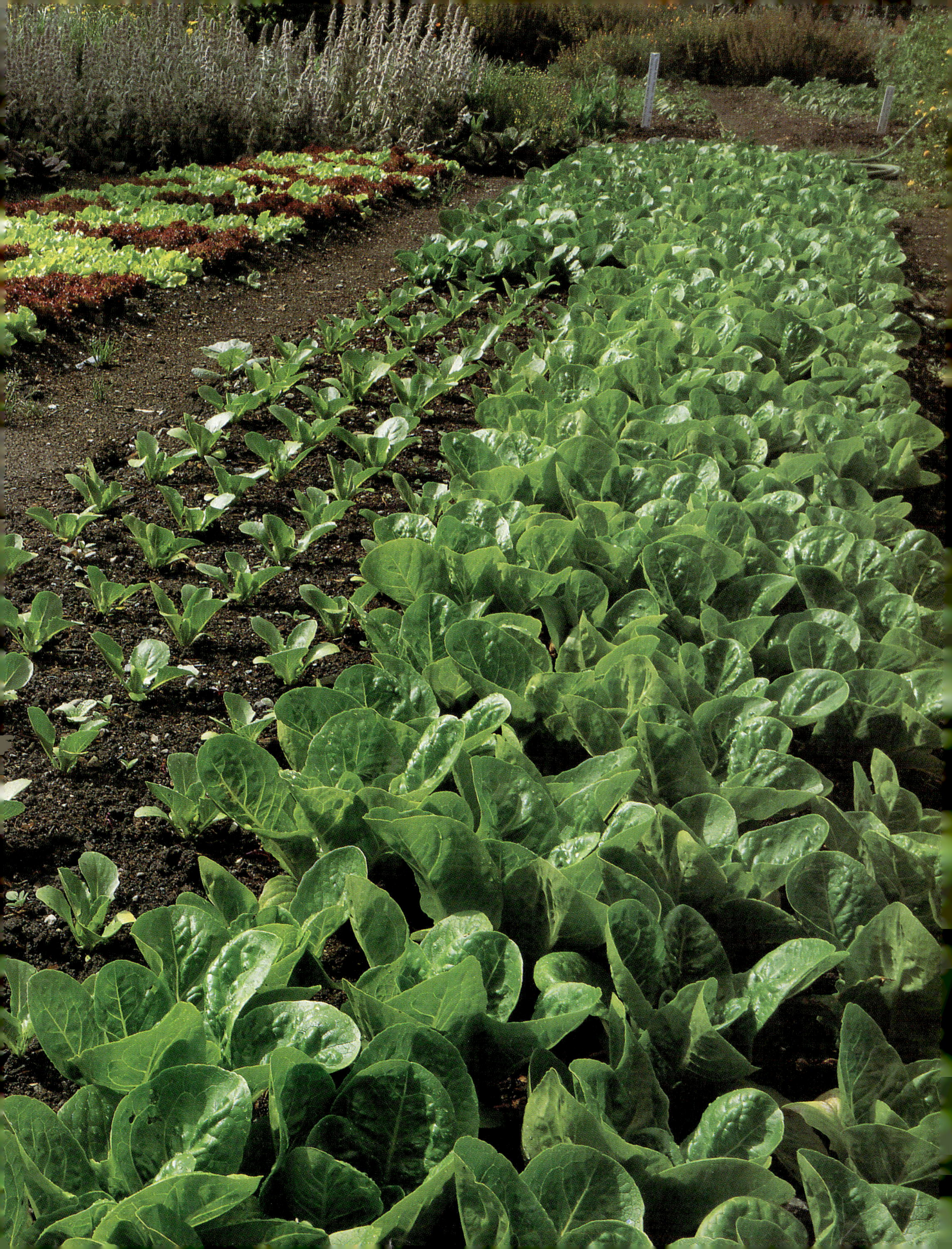

Garden Fresh Vegetables

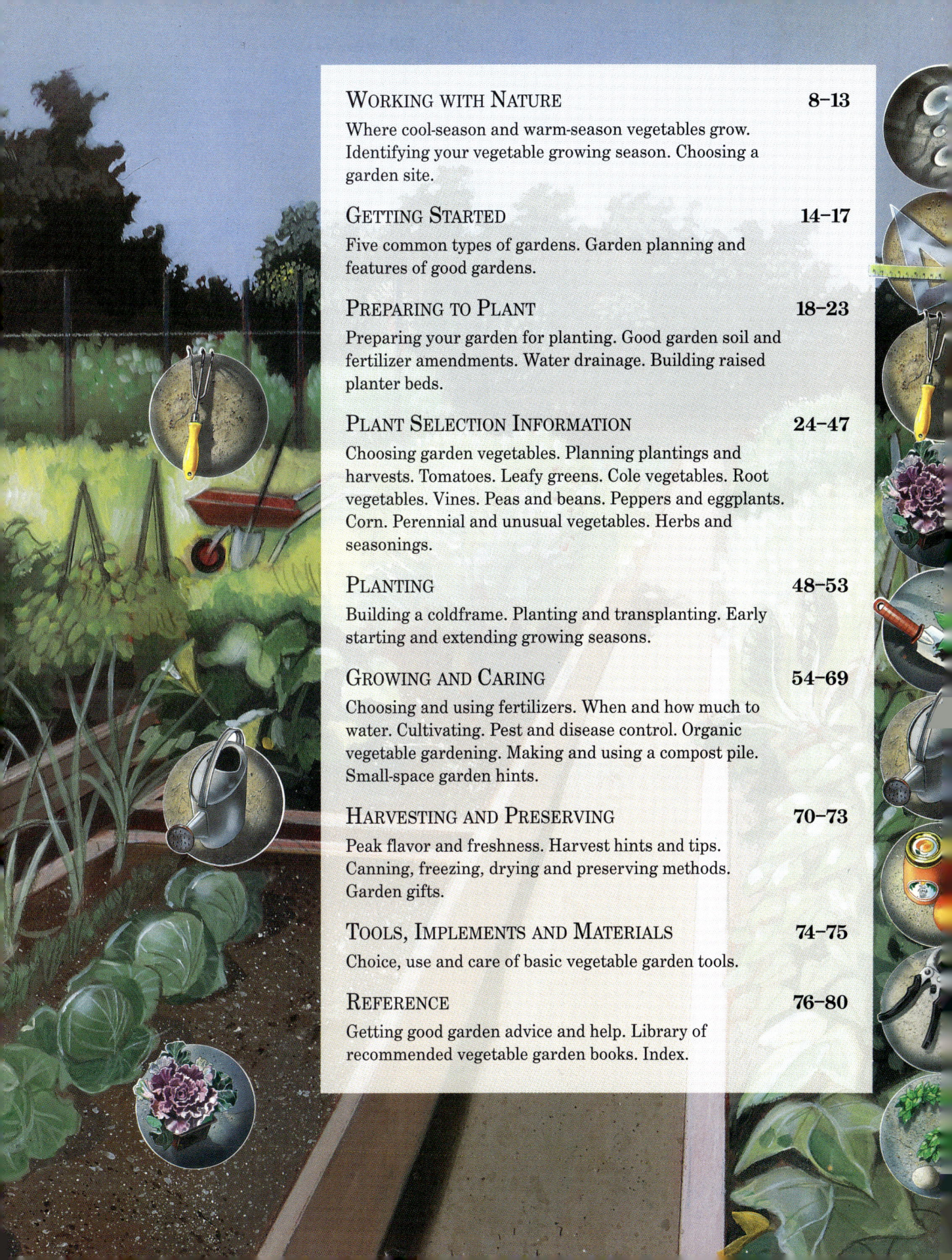

Working with Nature — 8–13
Where cool-season and warm-season vegetables grow. Identifying your vegetable growing season. Choosing a garden site.

Getting Started — 14–17
Five common types of gardens. Garden planning and features of good gardens.

Preparing to Plant — 18–23
Preparing your garden for planting. Good garden soil and fertilizer amendments. Water drainage. Building raised planter beds.

Plant Selection Information — 24–47
Choosing garden vegetables. Planning plantings and harvests. Tomatoes. Leafy greens. Cole vegetables. Root vegetables. Vines. Peas and beans. Peppers and eggplants. Corn. Perennial and unusual vegetables. Herbs and seasonings.

Planting — 48–53
Building a coldframe. Planting and transplanting. Early starting and extending growing seasons.

Growing and Caring — 54–69
Choosing and using fertilizers. When and how much to water. Cultivating. Pest and disease control. Organic vegetable gardening. Making and using a compost pile. Small-space garden hints.

Harvesting and Preserving — 70–73
Peak flavor and freshness. Harvest hints and tips. Canning, freezing, drying and preserving methods. Garden gifts.

Tools, Implements and Materials — 74–75
Choice, use and care of basic vegetable garden tools.

Reference — 76–80
Getting good garden advice and help. Library of recommended vegetable garden books. Index.

Your Climate and Growing Zones

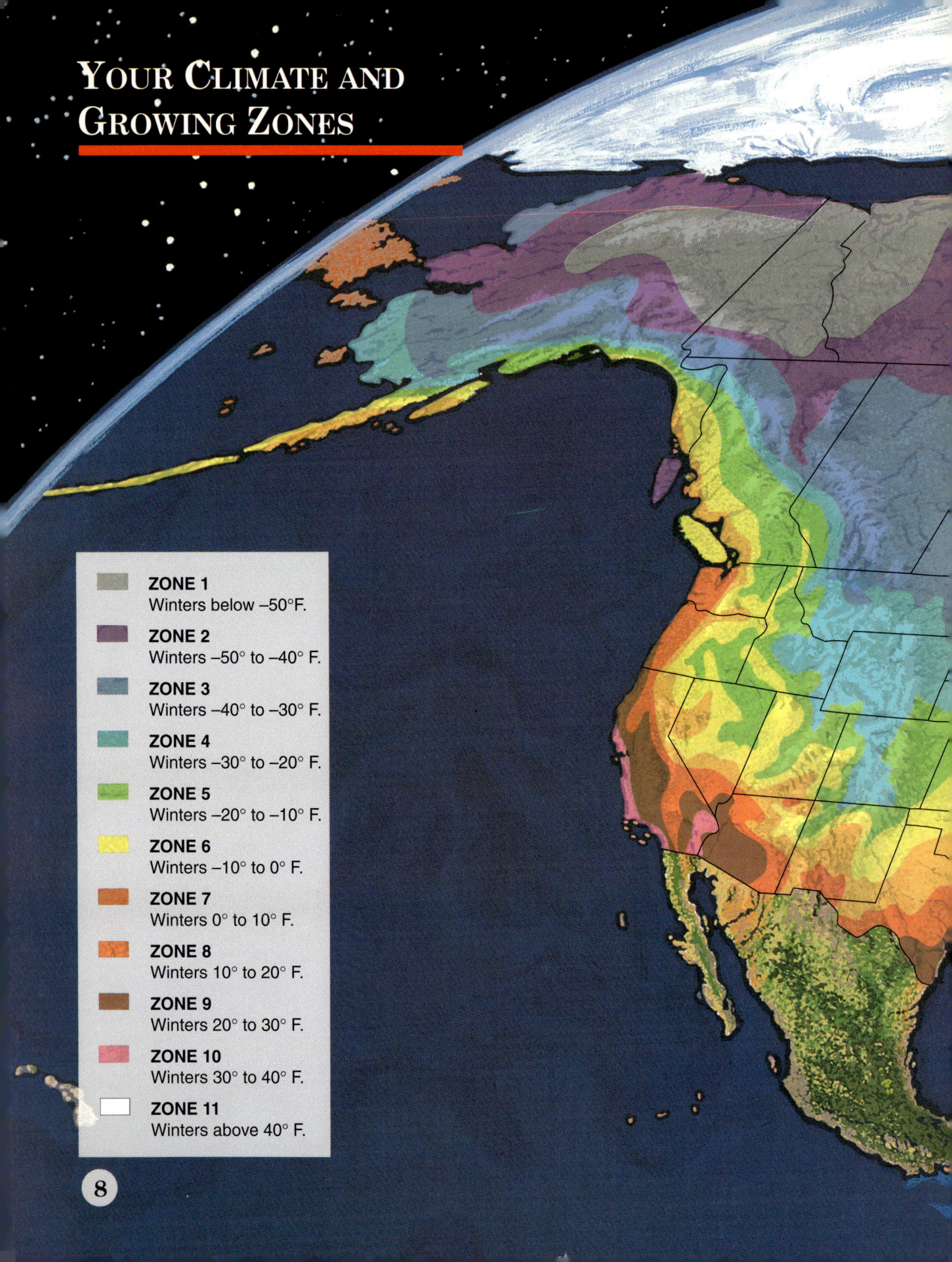

ZONE 1
Winters below −50°F.

ZONE 2
Winters −50° to −40° F.

ZONE 3
Winters −40° to −30° F.

ZONE 4
Winters −30° to −20° F.

ZONE 5
Winters −20° to −10° F.

ZONE 6
Winters −10° to 0° F.

ZONE 7
Winters 0° to 10° F.

ZONE 8
Winters 10° to 20° F.

ZONE 9
Winters 20° to 30° F.

ZONE 10
Winters 30° to 40° F.

ZONE 11
Winters above 40° F.

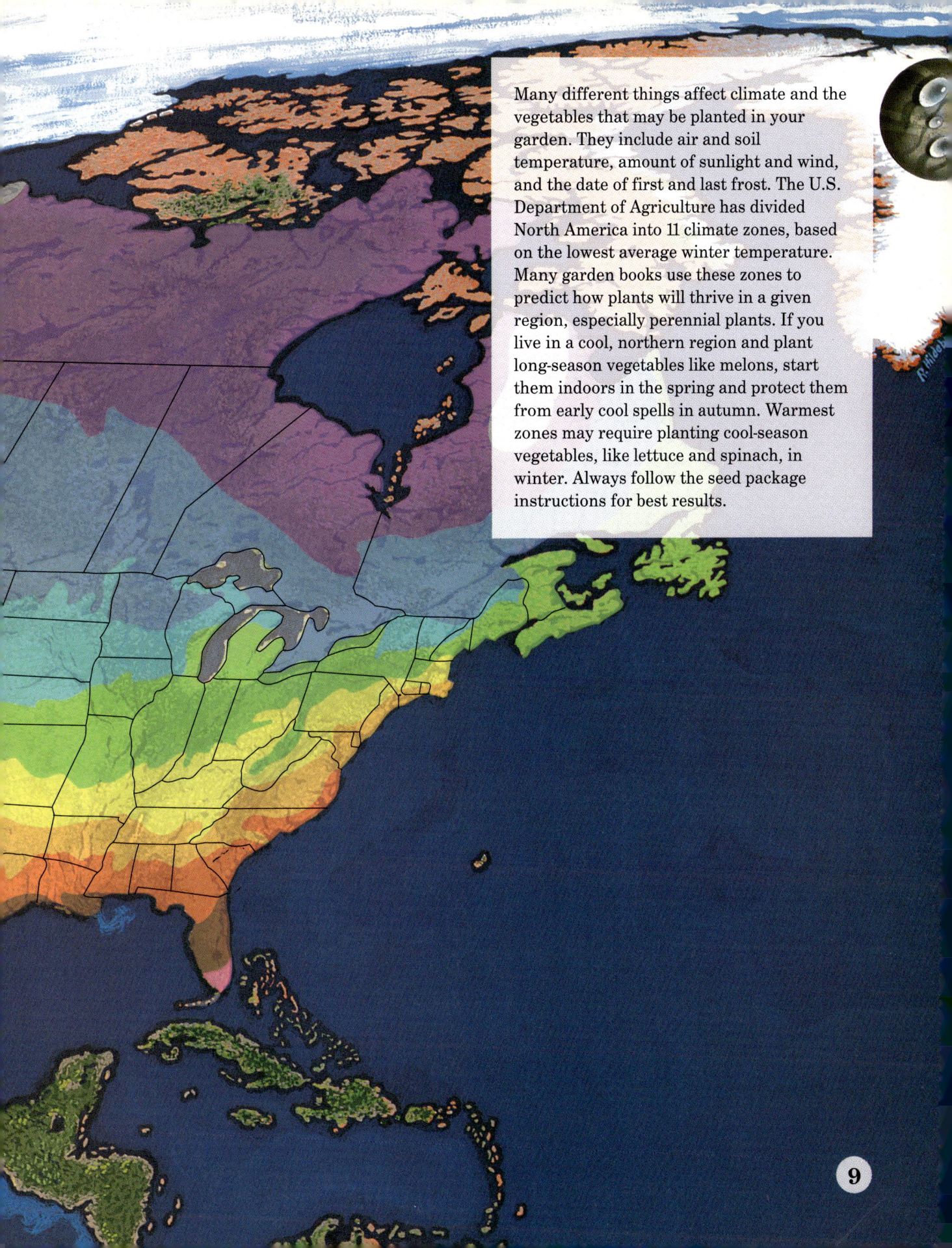

Many different things affect climate and the vegetables that may be planted in your garden. They include air and soil temperature, amount of sunlight and wind, and the date of first and last frost. The U.S. Department of Agriculture has divided North America into 11 climate zones, based on the lowest average winter temperature. Many garden books use these zones to predict how plants will thrive in a given region, especially perennial plants. If you live in a cool, northern region and plant long-season vegetables like melons, start them indoors in the spring and protect them from early cool spells in autumn. Warmest zones may require planting cool-season vegetables, like lettuce and spinach, in winter. Always follow the seed package instructions for best results.

Planting Zones Map

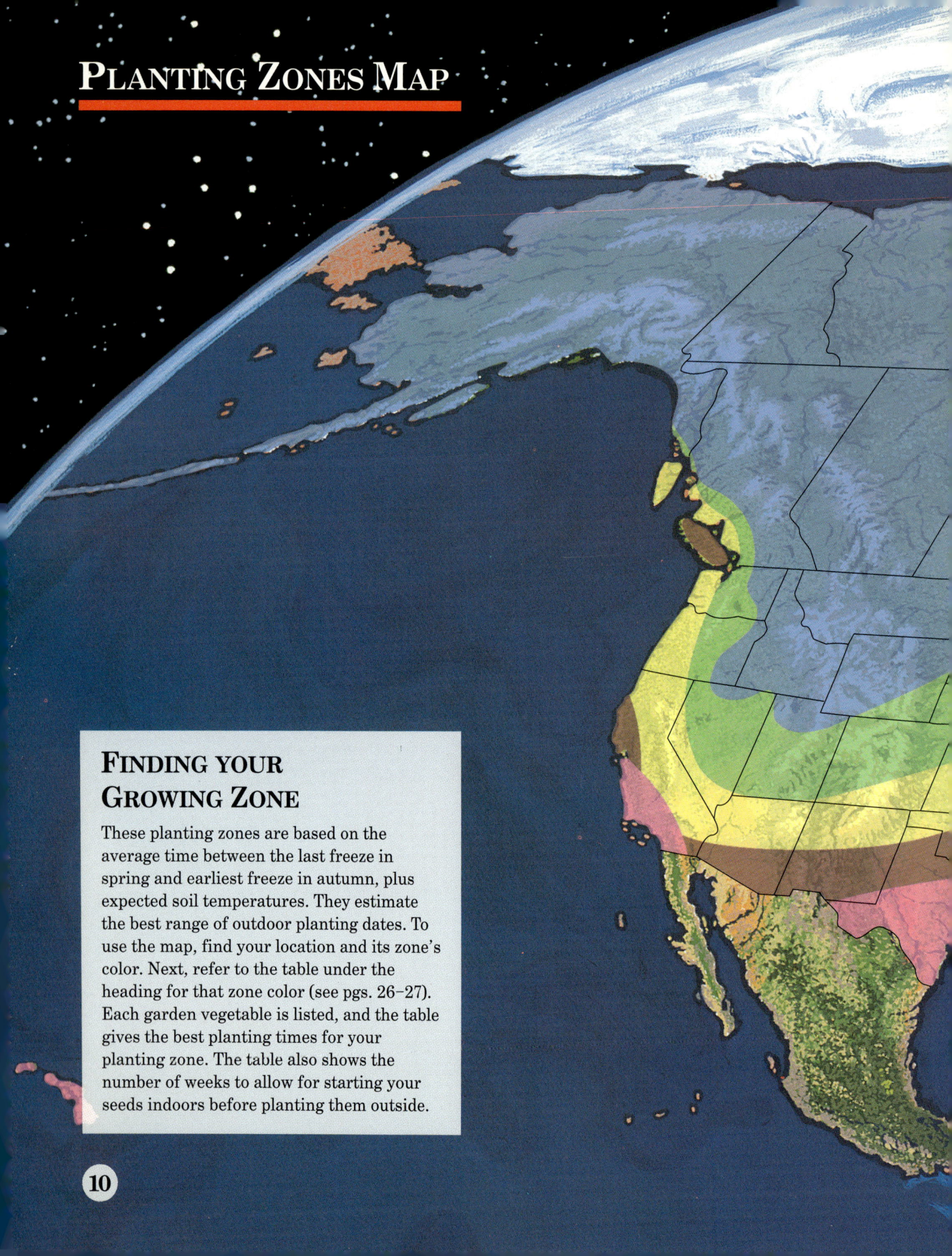

Finding your Growing Zone

These planting zones are based on the average time between the last freeze in spring and earliest freeze in autumn, plus expected soil temperatures. They estimate the best range of outdoor planting dates. To use the map, find your location and its zone's color. Next, refer to the table under the heading for that zone color (see pgs. 26–27). Each garden vegetable is listed, and the table gives the best planting times for your planting zone. The table also shows the number of weeks to allow for starting your seeds indoors before planting them outside.

WHEN TO PLANT OUTDOORS:

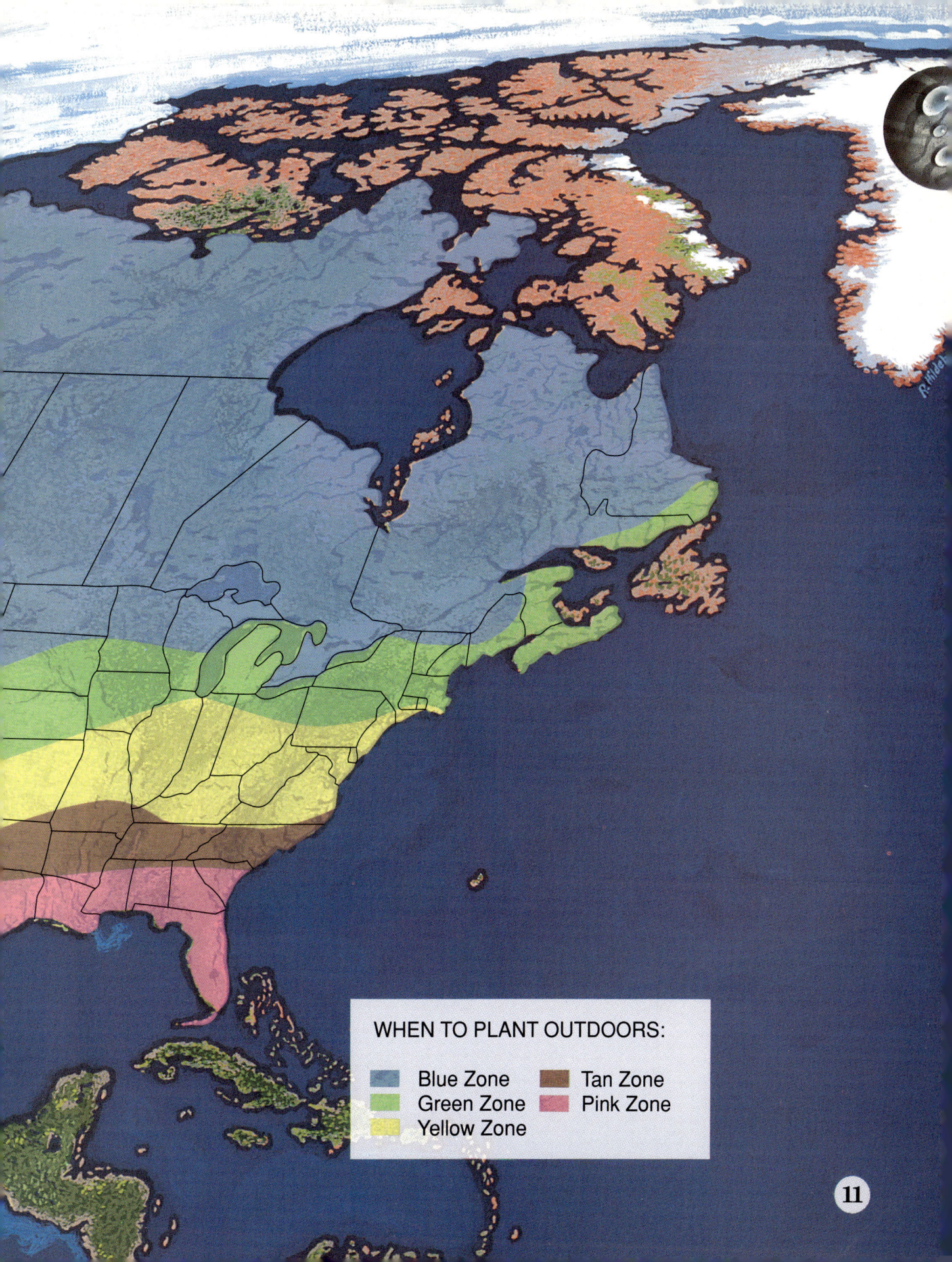

- Blue Zone
- Green Zone
- Yellow Zone
- Tan Zone
- Pink Zone

Garden Sites

Your garden location should have full sunlight throughout most daylight hours, shelter from constant wind and easy access to water. Hillsides often make good garden sites when they are terraced with low retaining walls into "benches" of level ground. Avoid low spots that may drain poorly and areas shaded by overhead trees or nearby buildings.

Hillside slopes sometimes have constant winds.

Observe sunlight on site all day. Avoid shadowed areas.

Poor, shady location.

Good hillside garden location.

Provide shelter from wind or choose wind-free location.

Good row garden site.

Space For Gardens

Family Size	Garden Size
2	200 sq. ft./20 m^2
4	350 sq. ft./35 m^2
6	500 sq. ft./50 m^2

FIVE GARDEN TYPES

The site you choose and the amount of space available will establish your garden type. Shown here are five popular gardens. Each is suited to its site and will produce vegetables of good quality and amount. Choose the garden type that best fits your location.

Terrace Garden. Garden walls hold flat benches of soil and slow water runoff.

Raised Bed Garden. Good where space is small, soil is poor or large yields per sq. ft. is desired.

Small-Space Garden. Tiny areas produce planned portions of selected fresh vegetables.

Flat rows. Traditional row vegetables for those blessed with flat sites and ample space.

Container Garden. For city dwellers with green thumbs or country kitchens.

Garden Planning

While no garden has all these features, good gardens have easy-to-reach planting beds divided by nonslip paths. The soil is loose, well-drained and rich with decomposed plant material and fertilizer. The best garden soil is prepared before planting season by adding compost and fertilizer to native soils of mixed clay, silt, sand and humus. Improve poorer soils by working in a 6–8 in. layer of compost. The prepared planting bed should be 2–3 ft. deep, allowing enough room for deep-rooted plants such as tomatoes. Install water supply pipes deep beneath paths for easy access and to avoid damage from garden tools or winter freezes.

Humus, soil and compost

Path

Planting bed

Frost zone

17

Preparing to Plant

All healthy plants need light, air, water and nutrients. Soil that is too dense may not let water and air reach the plant. Soils should be neither too acidic nor too alkaline (pH 6.0–7.5). Vegetable gardens need enough nutrients, even though only tiny amounts are used each day. Nitrogen is needed for proper growth of leaves. Phosphorus helps plants grow strong and fast, and potassium is needed for good root development.

The purple cast and dull color green in these plant leaves were caused by too little phosphorus. Add bone meal and superphosphate, both good sources of this long-lasting nutrient.

Lack of nitrogen can be seen in yellow leaves and stunted growth. Add blood meal, fish meal, rotted manure or a synthetic nitrogen fertilizer. Too much nitrogen can cause fertilizer burn, spindly growth and prevent the plant from flowering.

ORGANIC FERTILIZERS

Cottonseed meal

Bone meal

Blood meal

Hoof-and-horn meal

Fish meal

Fish emulsion

Composted manure

Potash

Wood ashes

Choosing Fertilizer

Vegetables grow, flower and fruit for a long time, and their quality, quantity and flavor can be affected by lack of food and water at any time during their growth.

Add fertilizers before planting and in regular, smaller doses throughout the growing season until harvest.

If you are unsure what fertilizer to use or have never planted in an area before, an inexpensive soil test will guide you (ask your local Agricultural Extension Service, garden stores or nurseries). Follow the label carefully for best results.

All fertilizers are labeled using an N–P–K code for the percentage by weight they contain of nitrogen (N), phosphorus (P) and potassium (K). The first number refers to nitrogen, the second to phosphorus, and the last to potassium, always in the same order.

Many organic fertilizers contain only one or two nutrients. Fertilizers with all three are called "complete," and those with equal amounts are called "balanced."

Watch your plants for early signs of stunted growth or yellowing. Prepare soil for planting in the spring by digging in a balanced or high-phosphorus fertilizer at the label-recommended rate.

Mottled leaves with darkened edges and stunted growth are signs of low potassium. Apply wood ash, pulverized granite, potash or a high-potassium synthetic. Fertilizer burn is unlikely.

SYNTHETIC FERTILIZERS

Ammonium nitrate

Ammonium sulfate

Calcium nitrate

Urea

Phosphoric acid

Superphosphate

Potassium chloride

Potassium nitrate

Potassium sulfate

Good Garden Soil

All garden soils are mixtures of clay, silt, sand and loam. Soils with too much clay are dense, hard to work and drain poorly. Sandy soils are too loose and dry out quickly. The best garden soils—loams and humus—combine all three with decayed plant matter, are easy to work and hold water and air.

Silt is larger than clay and smaller than sand, 1/100–1/10,000 of an inch. It retains water well, but lacks important air space between particles.

Clay particles are dustlike, less than 1/10,000 of an inch in diameter. Wet clay is sticky and hard to work. Dry clay is hard, locking out air and water.

Loam contains nearly equal parts of clay, silt and sand. It is the finest, most easily worked soil. It holds water, air and nutrients easily.

Sand has the largest soil particles, 1/25–1/100 of an inch. It contains lots of airspace but holds water and nutrients poorly.

IDEAL GARDEN SOIL

Check your soil drainage. Dig a hole in undisturbed soil that has not been watered or rained on for at least a week. The hole should be 1 ft. wide and 1 ft. deep. Fill it with water. Measure how long it takes for the water to completely soak in.

If it drains in less than 5 minutes, it is loose and sandy. If it takes more than 15 minutes, it is dense clay. Between 5 and 15 minutes is about right.

Improve both sandy and heavy clay soil by working in organic amendments like well-rotted compost or manure, peat moss, ground bark or sawdust. About 1/3 of the final soil mix should be amendment.

Clench a handful of soil in your palm. When released, it should crumble slowly in your hand, not stay in a ball or fall apart.

Raised-Bed Planters

Building raised-bed planters has many rewards. They give your garden a neat, attractive look and easier care. Europeans often use these "French intensive gardens" to overcome a shortage of garden space. They are easy answers to hopeless soils, since you can completely ignore the native soil and fill the planters with rich loam. Follow these simple instructions for a great garden.

MATERIALS

String, stakes for marking (Or use garden lime)

Spade or shovel

Garden tiller (Optional)

Wheelbarrow

2 x 12 green redwood or cedar lumber (Linear feet of bed perimeter)

1 x 3 2 ft. redwood or cedar stakes (2 per corner plus one each 16 in.)

1/4 x 3 lag screws (2 per stake plus 3 per corner)

First Choose your site and mark its border. Use stakes and string or a trail of garden lime. Remove any weeds or turf.

Third Locate bottom of edge boards 2 in. under outside ground surface. Drive stakes every 16 in. on inside. Fasten with lag screws.

Then Either till soil in bed until loose or remove top 18 in. for replacement. Trench the marked border with a shovel.

Last Backfill bed with well-rotted compost and added fertilizer. Dig deeply (18–24 in.) to thoroughly mix with native soil, rake.

CAUTION

Never use preservative-treated lumber for vegetable gardens.

VEGETABLE CHOICES

Once garden construction ends and frost danger passes, planting starts. Cool-season plants are first. They prefer cool soil and short days. Warm-season plantings soon follow. Most gardeners choose their plants by expected results: crisp, crunchy salads, full-flavored table or cooking vegetables, preserves and canned vegetables, or specialty vegetables, such as those for oriental cooking or Tex-Mex Southwest flavors. Pages 26–47 show most garden vegetable choices.

TABLE VEGETABLES
Savory green beans, plump peas, broccoli and cauliflower, beets and corn on the cob.

SALAD VEGETABLES
Crunchy, tasty salads of crisp lettuce and spinach, cucumber, radishes, juicy tomatoes and sweet onions.

PRESERVING VEGETABLES
Sweet and dill pickles, dried beans and blackeyed peas, sweet wax peppers, sunflower seeds and popcorn.

FULL SEASON VEGETABLES
Cantaloupes, honeydew melons, sweet corn, pumpkins and winter squash.

Planning Plantings and Harvests

Everything needed to plant common garden vegetables is found here. For each plant, the following information is given: Vegetable name; Page shown in book (pgs. 28–47); Type (cool- or warm-season, perennial or bulb); Minimum and Ideal soil planting temperatures; Depth to Plant; Spacing of Plants, Rows and Hills; Seed Germination Time; Planting Dates (see Map on pgs. 10–11); and Days until Harvest.

Vegetable	Page	Type	Soil Temp—Min	Soil Temp—Ideal	Plant Depth (in.)	Spacing Plants–Rows (in.)	Spacing Plants–Plants (in.)	Spacing Plants–Hill (in.)	Days to Germination	Blue Zone	Green Zone	Yellow Zone	Tan Zone	Pink Zone	Days to Harvest
Amaranth	31	WS	60	80	1/4	24	24		10–12	May–Jun	May	Apr	Apr	Mar	40–56
Artichoke	44	CSP	40	70	1/2	72–94	48–72			Jun	May–Jun	Apr–Jun	Sep–Mar	Oct–Feb	Perennial
Asparagus	44	CSP	50	75	1/2	24	18		14–21	May–Jun	May	Apr	Apr	Mar	Perennial
Bean, Broad	38	WS	60	80	1–1 1/2	36	6		7–10	Jun	May–Jun	May–Jun	Apr–Jun	Mar–Aug	66
Bean, Lima	38	WS	60	80	1 1/2	36	3		7–10	Jun	May–Jun	May–Jun	Apr–Jun	Mar–Aug	65
Bean, Runner	38	WS	60	80	1 1/2–2	36–48	3		8–12	Jun	May–Jun	Apr–Jun	Apr–Aug	Mar–Aug	45–70
Bean, Snap	38	WS	60	85	1–1 1/2	18	3		7–10	Jun	May–Jun	May–Jun	Apr–Jun	Mar–Aug	54
Bean–Asparagus	38	WS	60	80	1–1 1/2	36	6		7–10	Jun	May–Jun	May–Jun	Apr–Jun	Mar–Aug	75
Beet	34	CS	40	85	1/2	18	1 1/2		10–12	May–Jul	Apr–Jul	Mar–Jul	Feb–Oct	Jan–Dec	58
Broccoli	32	CS	40	85	1/2	36	18		10–15	May–Jun	Apr–May	Mar–Apr	Feb–Apr	Jul–Oct	85
Brussels Sprouts	32	CS	40	85	1/4	36	24		10–15	May	Apr–May	Mar–Apr	Feb–Apr	Jul–Oct	100
Cabbage	32	CS	40	85	1/2	30	18		10–15	May	Apr–May	Mar–Apr	Feb–Apr	Sep–Feb	76
Cabbage, Chinese	32	CS	40	85	1/2	30	18		10–15	May	Apr–May	Mar–Apr	Feb–Apr	Sep–Feb	75
Cantaloupe	36	WS	60	95	1/2	48		48	5–10	Jun	May–Jun	Apr–Jun	Apr–Jun	Apr–Jun	86
Cardoon	NA	WSP	60	80	1/2	36	20		10–15	Jun	May–Jun	Apr–Jun	Sep–Mar	Oct–Feb	Perennial
Carrot	34	CS	40	80	1/4–1/2	12	2		14–25	May–Jun	Apr–Jun	Mar–Jun	Jan–Mar	Jan–Dec	68
Cauliflower	32	CS	40	80	1/2	36	18		8–10	May	Apr–May	Mar–Apr	Feb–Mar	Jul–Oct	70
Celery	NA	CS	40	70	1/8	24	6–10		14–21		Apr–May	Mar–Apr	Feb–Apr	Jul–Oct	105–130
Collards	32	CS	45	85	1/4	36	18		10–15	May	Apr–May	Mar–Apr	Feb–Aug	Feb–Aug	75
Corn, Ornamental	42	WS	50	85	1	36	12		5–7	Jun	May–Jun	Apr–Jun	Mar–Jun	Mar–Jul	105
Corn, Popcorn	42	WS	50	85	1	36	20		7–10	Jun	May–Jun	May–Jul	Mar–Jun	Apr–Jun	85
Corn, Sweet	42	WS	50	85	1–1 1/2	36	20		7–10	Jun	May–Jun	May–Jul	Mar–Jun	Apr–Jun	77
Cress, Garden	30	CS	50	75	1/4	12–16	1–2		10–14	May–Jun	Apr–Jun	Mar–Jun	Aug–May	Sep–May	45–60
Cress, Watercress	NA	CS	50	75	1/8		2–4		7–10	May–Jun	Apr–Jun	Mar–Jun	Aug–May	Sep–May	50
Cucumber	36	WS	60	95	1/2	72		48	8–10	Jun	May–Jun	Apr–Jun	Apr–Jun	Apr–Jun	57
Eggplant	40	WS	70	85	1/4	36	15		10–15	Jun	May–Jun	Mar–May	Feb–Apr	Feb–Mar	80
Endive	30	CS	32	75	1/4	24	12		7–14	May	Apr–Jun	Mar–May	Aug–Sep	Jul–Sep	95
Garlic	34	Bulb	40	70	1 1/2	15	4–8			May	May–Jun	Apr–Jun	Mar–Jul	Sep–Mar	90–100
Gourd	36	WS	60	95	1		18	48	10–12	Jun	May–Jun	Apr–Jun	Apr–Jun	Mar–Jun	90
Greens	30	CS	40	70	1/4	18	6		10–14	May–Jun	Apr–Jun	Mar–Jun	Aug–May	Sep–May	40
Herb, Basil	46	WS	60	95	1/4		12		7–10	May–Jun	May–Jun	Apr–May	Feb–Mar	Jan–Mar	30
Herb, Caraway	46	WS	60	95	1/4	12–18	6–8		14–18	May–Jun	May–Jun	Apr–May	Feb–Mar	Jan–Mar	Biennial
Herb, Catnip	46	WS	60	95	1/4	16	12		8–10	May–Jun	May–Jun	Apr–May	Feb–Mar	Jan–Mar	50–60
Herb, Chervil	46	WS	55	85	1/4	8	8–14			May–Jun	May–Jun	Apr–May	Feb–Mar	Jan–Mar	40–60
Herb, Chinese Parsley	46	WS	60	80	1/2	18	8		10–14	May–Jun	Apr–Jun	Mar–Jun	Aug–May	Sep–May	40–45
Herb, Chives	46	WS	60	80	1/4	12	18		10–14	May–Jun	May–Jun	Apr–May	Feb–Mar	Jan–Mar	40–45
Herb, Cilantro	46	WS	60	80	1/4	8	18		14–18	May–Jun	May–Jun	Apr–May	Feb–Mar	Jan–Mar	35–40

Vegetable	Page	Type	Soil Temp–Min	Soil Temp–Ideal	Plant Depth (in.)	Spacing Plants–Rows (in.)	Spacing Plants–Plants (in.)	Spacing Plants–Hill (in.)	Days to Germination	Blue Zone	Green Zone	Yellow Zone	Tan Zone	Pink Zone	Days to Harvest
Herb, Coriander	46	WS	60	80	1/4	8	18		14-18	May-Jun	May-Jun	Apr-May	Feb-Mar	Jan-Mar	35-40
Herb, Dill	46	WS	60	75	1/8	8-12	18		21-25	May-Jun	May-Jun	Apr-May	Feb-Mar	Jan-Mar	25-30
Herb, Fennel	46	WSP	60	80	1/4	12	19		14-18	May-Jun	May-Jun	Apr-May	Feb-Mar	Jan-Mar	Perennial
Herb, Mints	46	WSP	60	80	1/4	12	12		12-16	May-Jun	May-Jun	Apr-May	Feb-Mar	Jan-Mar	Perennial
Herb, Oregano	46	WS	60	75	1/16	12	12		8-10	May-Jun	May-Jun	Apr-May	Feb-Mar	Jan-Mar	35
Herb, Parsley	46	CS	40	60	1/4	10	6		18-24	May-Jun	Apr-Jun	Mar-Jun	Aug-May	Sep-May	45-60
Herb, Parsley	46	WS	50	60	1/4	18	6		14-21	Apr-May	Apr-May	Mar-Apr	Sep-Oct	Oct-Nov	90
Herb, Sage	46	WS	50	60	1/4	12	12		14-21	May-Jun	May-Jun	Apr-May	Feb-Mar	Jan-Mar	35
Herb, Savory	46	WS	60	80	1/16	6	12		10-15	May-Jun	May-Jun	Apr-May	Feb-Mar	Jan-Mar	42
Herb, Sweet Marjoram	46	WS	60	65	1/4	8	6		8-10	May-Jun	May-Jun	Apr-May	Feb-Mar	Jan-Mar	40-45
Kale	32	CS	40	75	1/4	18	12		10-14	May	Apr-May	Mar-Apr	Feb-Mar	Sep-Apr	55
Kohlrabi	32	CS	40	75	1/2	18	6		12-15	May-Jun	May-Jul	Mar-Aug	Feb-Sep	Jan-Dec	45-60
Leek	34	CS	40	75	1/2	18	6		10-14	May	Apr-May	Feb-May	Dec-Apr	Sep-May	150
Lettuce	30	CS	32	75	1/4	12	10		7-10	May-Jun	Apr-Jun	Mar-Jun	Aug-May	Sep-May	45
Melon	36	WS	60	95	1/2	48		48	5-10	Jun	May-Jun	Apr-Jun	Apr-Jun	Apr-Jun	110
Mustard	30	CS	40	75	1/4	15	12		8-9	Jun	May-Jul	Mar-Jun	Feb-May	Feb-Mar	45
Mustard Spinach	30	CS	40	75	1/4	12	10		9-12	Jun	May-Jul	Mar-Sep	Feb-Oct	Jan-Dec	30
Mustard, India	30	CS	50	80	1/4	12	10		9-12	Jun	May-Jul	Mar-Sep	Feb-Oct	Jan-Dec	30
Okra	38	CS	60	95	3/4	36	18		10-14	Jun	May-Jun	Apr-Jun	Apr-Jun	Apr-Jun	56
Onion, Drying	34	Bulb	32	80	1/2	18	6		12-14	May-Jun	Apr-Jun	Feb-May	Dec-Apr	Dec-Mar	110
Onion, Green	34	CS	32	80	1/2	12	2		12-14	May-Jun	Apr-Jun	Feb-May	Dec-Apr	Jan-Dec	60-110
Parsnip	34	CS	32	70	1/2	18	3		21-28	May-Jun	May-Jun	Apr-Jun	Feb-Jun	Mar-Jun	95
Pea, English Garden	38	CS	40	75	1 1/2	30	2		8-12	May	Apr-May	Feb-Apr	Jan-Sep	Jan-Sep	60
Pea, Snap	38	CS	40	75	1 1/2	30	2		6-10	May	Apr-May	Feb-Apr	Jan-Sep	Jan-Sep	70
Pea, Southern (Cowpea)	38	WS	60	85	1/2-1	36	3		7-10	Jun	May-Jun	May-Jun	Apr-Jun	Mar-Aug	78
Pepper, Chili	40	WS	60	85	1/4	24	18		10-12	Jun	May-Jun	Mar-May	Feb-Apr	Feb-Mar	80
Pepper, Sweet	40	WS	60	85	1/4	24	18		10-12	Jun	May-Jun	Mar-May	Feb-Apr	Feb-Mar	70
Potato, Sweet	34	WS	60	85	2-3	36-48	10-18	36		May-Jun	Apr-Jun	Mar-Jul	Mar-Aug	Feb-Sep	110-120
Potatoes	34	CS	40	75	2-3	36-48	10-18	36		May	Apr-Jun	Mar-Jun	Feb-May	Oct-Feb	110-120
Pumpkin	36	WS	60	95	1 1/2	96		96	8-10	Jun	May-Jun	Apr-Jun	Apr-Jun	Apr-Jun	120
Radish	34	CS	40	85	1/2	10	1		4-6	May-Jul	Apr-Jul	Mar-Aug	Feb-Oct	Jan-Dec	26
Rhubarb	44	CSP	50	75	1	36		48	14-21	Apr-Jun	Apr-Jun	Mar-Jun	Sep-Feb	Oct-Feb	Perennial
Roquette	30	CS	50	60	1/2	16	6-8		5-8	May-Jul	Apr-Jul	Mar-Jul	Aug-May	Sep-May	35
Rutabaga	34	CS	40	85	1/2	18	8		7-10	Jun	Jun	Jul	Aug	Sep	90
Salsify	34	CS	40	80	1/2-1	18	4		14-20	May	Apr-May	Apr	Jun	Jun	120
Shallot	34	Bulb	60	75	1/2	24-48	4-8		18	May-Jun	Apr-Jun	Feb-May	Dec-Apr	Dec-Mar	60-120
Sorrel	44	WSP	65	75	1/4	18	1		7-10	Jun	May-Jun	May-Jun	Apr-Jun	Mar-Aug	Perennial
Soybean	38	WS	60	95	1-1 1/2	18	3		7-10	Jun	May-Jun	May-Jun	Apr-Jun	Mar-Aug	85
Spinach, New Zealand	30	WS	60	80	1	24	12		14-20	Jun	May-Jun	Apr-Jun	Apr-Jun	Apr-Jun	70
Spinach, True	30	CS	32	70	1/2	18	6		8-10	May-Jun	Apr-Jun	Mar-Jun	Aug-May	Sep-May	45
Squash, Summer	36	WS	60	95	1	48-60	48	48	8-10	Jun	May-Jun	Apr-Jun	Apr-Jun	Apr-Jun	50
Squash, Winter	36	WS	60	95	1 1/2	48-60	96	72	8-10	Jun	May-Jun	Apr-Jun	Apr-Jun	Apr-Jun	120
Sunflower	44	WS	60	95	1		18-24		10-14	May-Jun	May-Jun	Apr-Jun	Mar-Jun	Mar-Jul	68-80
Swiss Chard	30	CS	40	85	3/4	18	6		7-10	May-Jun	Apr-Jul	Mar-Aug	Feb-Sep	Jan-Dec	60
Tomatillo	44	WS	60	85	1/4	24	24		8-10	Jun	May-Jun	Apr-May	Feb-Mar	Jan-Mar	95
Tomato	28	WS	50	85	1/4	24	24		8-10	Jun	May-Jun	Apr-May	Feb-Mar	Jan-Mar	80
Turnip	34	CS	40	85	1/2	15	4		8-12	May-Jun	Apr-Jun	Mar-Jun	Aug-May	Sep-May	45
Watermelon	36	WS	60	95	1/2	72		48	5-7	Jun	May-Jun	Apr-Jun	Apr-Jun	Apr-Jun	73

TOMATOES

Whether grown for eating, juicing, slicing, appetizers, sauces or preserves, tomatoes are an easy success in nearly every garden. Colors range from red and yellow, to green and striped. Harvest in 60–82 days, depending on variety

CHERRIES AND PEARS
Bite-sized salad and appetizer favorites with rich taste.

YELLOW TOMATOES
Add colorful excitement to your table and meals.

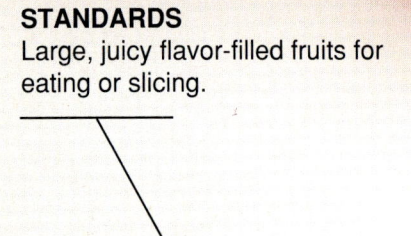

STANDARDS
Large, juicy flavor-filled fruits for eating or slicing.

PASTE TOMATOES
Dense, meaty tomatoes for cooking and drying.

SPECIALTY TOMATOES
Unusual Costoluto Genovese, Marvel Stripe, Peach or Zebra.

ABOUT TOMATOES

Special tomatoes have been developed for different uses, as well as for special climate needs and for disease tolerance.

Choose either *determinate* or *indeterminate* plants. Determinate plants are bushier, ripen all their fruit at the same time and have flowers only on the ends of main stems. Indeterminate plants flower repeatedly on branch stems, grow taller and bear fruit until killed by frost.

Plant early varieties if summer nights are generally cooler than 60° F or you want an early harvest. Choose disease-resistant varieties marked V, F, N or T for resistance to verticillium, fusarium, nematodes or tobacco mosaic virus.

Start seedlings indoors in a sunny place 4–5 weeks before planting outdoors. Seeds planted 1/4 in. deep should germinate in 8–10 days. Transplant outside when seedlings have 5–6 leaves. Bury the stem up to the first real leaves. Allow 24 in. between each plant and row. Fertilize every 4–6 weeks throughout the growing season.

To keep fruit clean and make harvest easier, support plants with stakes or cages.

Leafy Green Vegetables

Tender, mouth-watering and colorful, salads and cooked greens are the first prize of cool-season gardens. Besides many endive, spinach and lettuce options, add peppery and surprising tastes with roquette, mustard and mustard spinach. Or make meals a real treat with fresh cooked greens.

LETTUCE
Crisphead, straight or curly leaf, butterhead, cos (romaine) or endive.

SPINACH
Plant early, then again in late summer for fall harvests.

MUSTARDS
Tastes range from spinach to cabbage. For salads or cooking.

ROQUETTE
Peppery flavor for salads, soups or cooked greens.

SWISS CHARD
Use leaves like summer spinach. Stems cook like asparagus.

MIXED GREENS
Chop suey greens (edible chrysanthemum), turnip greens, amaranth, chicory, cress.

COLE VEGETABLES

Rich-flavored and delicious raw or cooked, these garden favorites make meals come alive. All love cool weather and are easy to grow. Pick them early for tenderness.

CHINESE CABBAGE
Whether used fresh in salads or stir-fried, a tasty treat.

KALE AND COLLARDS
Salad greens, garnishes, or terrific cooked greens.

BRUSSELS SPROUTS
Pick 1/4-in. wide sprouts from bottom of stem.

BROCCOLI
Cut main head early and pick tender side shoots until frost.

CABBAGE
Red, smooth or crinkled, for salads, coleslaw or cooking.

CAULIFLOWER
Tie outer leaves over forming heads to make them white.

KOHLRABI
Serve sliced with dip or steamed like cauliflower.

33

ROOT VEGETABLES

From early spring through winter, root vegetables bring fresh taste to the table. Eaten raw, cooked, pickled or preserved, their rich flavors and simple care during growth make them popular for gardeners and cooks alike. Choose from familiar and unusual vegetable varieties.

BEETS
Excellent for eating fresh, canning, pickling or freezing.

RADISHES
From giants to salad varieties, zesty taste.

CARROTS
Snapping crisp in short, slender and miniature varieties.

ONIONS, SHALLOTS AND LEEKS
Use green, sliced or cooked, choice of mild or hardy flavors.

PARSNIP, PARSLEY AND SALSIFY
Unique, old-world flavors. Taste sweetest after frost.

TURNIP AND RUTABAGA
Serve boiled with butter, mashed or in soups and stews.

GARLIC
Make showy braids for welcome kitchen gifts with sharp flavor.

POTATOES AND SWEET POTATOES
Pick red, yellow, white and purple potatoes, or yellow or white sweet potatoes.

Vine Plants

Gardens with vine plants provide colorful flowers and foliage all summer long, as well as delicious fruit. Eat some fresh from the vine, preserve others, store some for winter treats and display the rest—vines provide a bounty of vegetables!

CANTALOUPES AND MELONS
Muskmelons, watermelons, honeydews and cantaloupes say summer sweetness.

CUCUMBERS
Pick from oriental, middle-eastern, pickling, slicing, burpless or lemon cucumbers.

PUMPKINS AND GOURDS
Choose from 8 oz. to 100 lb. pumpkin varieties—ornamental, birdhouse and luffa-sponge gourds.

SUMMER SQUASH
Zucchini, straightneck, crookneck, cocozelle (marrow) and scallop.

WINTER SQUASH
Hard outer shell protects sweet, nutty flavor throughout winter storage.

Peas, Beans and Okra

Quick to sprout and onto your table, peas and beans provide many choices for fresh eating, canning, freezing and drying. Their beautiful leaves and striking flowers are lovely to look at, while promising fresh taste treats to come.

SPECIALTY BEANS
Soybeans, wax, lima, romano, purple pod, asparagus and scarlet runner beans.

GREEN SNAP BEANS
Pole and bush, stringed or stringless.

OKRA
Cooked, fried, pickled or in soups, okra says "Southern."

SOUTHERN PEAS
Cowpeas, purple hulls, blackeye and crowder. Use fresh or dried.

EDIBLE-POD PEAS
Sugar sweet, snap-crisp and great for oriental cooking.

ENGLISH GARDEN PEAS
Delicious whether fresh, cooked alone or with other vegetables.

BUSH OR POLE?

A gardener's first question is whether to plant pole varieties or bush plants.

Space-saving pole beans and peas produce longer but require extra work when planting. Some prefer their flavor and taste to bush plants, they are easier to harvest.

Bush plants can be started earlier, are hardier, but yield less than pole varieties. Some varieties also bear smaller pods than the pole varieties.

Best of the pole beans are Blue Lake, Kentucky Wonder and Kentucky Blue snap beans and Romano broad beans. For bush beans choose Dandy, Blue Lake 274 and Greencrop snaps, Roma II broads and Royalty Purple with unusual pods that turn from purple to green when cooked.

Try Sparkle and Little Marvel garden peas, Sugar Ann and Sugar Snap edible-pod peas, and Pinkeye, California Blackeye and Asparagus cowpeas.

Install 9-ft. tall poles at planting time. or tall fences or a trellis will also give good support. Growing vines will follow a sturdy string from stakes at each plant to the top of the support.

Provide low supports of stakes and twine for bush peas and beans to make harvesting easier and to contain their growth.

PEPPERS AND EGGPLANTS

Peppers and eggplants suggest hot summer weather. They set fruit best when days are warm and nights cool only slightly. Whether you favor fiery south-of-the-border food or want garden memories of Italy and Greece, they will gather comments and applause.

JAPANESE EGGPLANT
Subtle flavors and thinnest skin make it tempura-perfect.

CHILI PEPPERS
From mild to amazingly hot. Water the evening before harvest for milder taste.

EGGPLANT
A Mediterranean-style cooking favorite, breaded and fried or baked alone or in casseroles.

SWEET PEPPERS
Bell, banana, cherry and pimiento in attractive green, yellow, red and purple.

Corn

Fresh-picked corn is the sweetest corn. Once picked, corn sugar turns to starch and flavor is lost. Be sure to plant enough short rows to form a block; corn won't pollinate without lots of neighboring plants. Plan on harvesting about one or two ears per plant.

POPCORN
Harvest before frost, dry 3 weeks. Twist off kernels or pop the whole ear.

ORNAMENTAL CORN
Festive decoration to grow with pumpkins and gourds. Choose inedible or popcorn varieties.

SWEET CORN
Enjoy corn all season long with early and late varieties. Try white, two-color or yellow.

Perennials and Unusual Vegetables

If you have the time and space, try perennial vegetables like artichokes, asparagus and rhubarb. Or gather a neighbor's praise with a stand of 8-ft. tall sunflowers. Grow husk tomatoes for an ice cream topping and tomatillos for salsa verde. Now you're gardening!

SUNFLOWER
Cut heads when backs yellow, hang upside-down indoors until dry, then remove seeds.

Artichokes Kin to thistles. Cut buds while young and tender. Boil and eat the leaves.

Rhubarb For sauces, toppings and pies. Three plants will keep everyone happy.

Asparagus Worth the wait: 3 years from seed to first yearly harvest, 2 years from crowns.

Tomatillo and Ground Cherry Tomatillo, cape gooseberry, strawberry or husk tomato.

Sorrel For salads with spinach texture and lemon-like bite, or cooked.

PLANTING PERENNIALS

Perennials give gardeners a nearly toil-free annual harvest once they begin to produce (2 to 3 years from planting).

While asparagus, artichokes and rhubarb can be planted from seed, most gardeners plant year-old crowns (rhizomes), available each spring, to shorten the long wait.

Asparagus Good preparation is the key to many years of production. Fill a 12-in. wide, 24-in. deep trench with 12–14 in. of loose compost or rotted manure. Form a central ridge, with the top about 10 in. below the soil's surface.

Place the crowns atop the ridge so that the roots dangle down each side. Space the plants 18 in. apart

Partially fill the trench with more compost. The crowns should be covered 2 in. deep. When shoots emerge add a little soil, without covering the shoot tips. Repeat every few days until the trench is filled.

Artichoke Prepare compost beds 12 in. deep for each root division. Space plants 4–6 ft. apart. Planted division should be 6–8 in. deep.

Rhubarb Prepare hills 36–48 in. apart with compost 12–18 in. deep. Plant crowns about 1 in. beneath the ground surface.

Herbs and Seasonings

CHERVIL
Mild flavor favored in French cuisine.

DILL
Use both seeds and leaves.

PARSLEY
Italian, Chinese or curled.

SUMMER SAVORY
Peppery in egg dishes, soups.

CARAWAY
Flowers yield edible seeds.

CHIVES
Grass-like onion-scented leaves.

BASIL
Sweet or spicy globe varieties.

CATNIP
Turns tabbies into tigers.

46

OREGANO
All-time Mediterranean favorite.

SAGE
Traditional for turkey dressing.

SWEET MARJORAM
Velvet, gray-green leaves.

FENNEL
Secret pizza ingredient.

CORIANDER
Cilantro to some, Chinese parsley to others.

PEPPERMINT
Grow in containers to control spreading.

OTHER COMMON GARDEN HERBS

Rosemary

Winter Savory

Thyme

Tarragon

SORREL
For lemon-flavored, spinach-like salads or cooked.

47

Building a Coldframe

Give warm-season vegetables an early start (see pg. 52) by using this quick-to-build coldframe made with common, low-cost materials. You'll harvest sooner and have stronger plants by protecting tender sprouts from frost or too-cold soil during their first few weeks of growth.

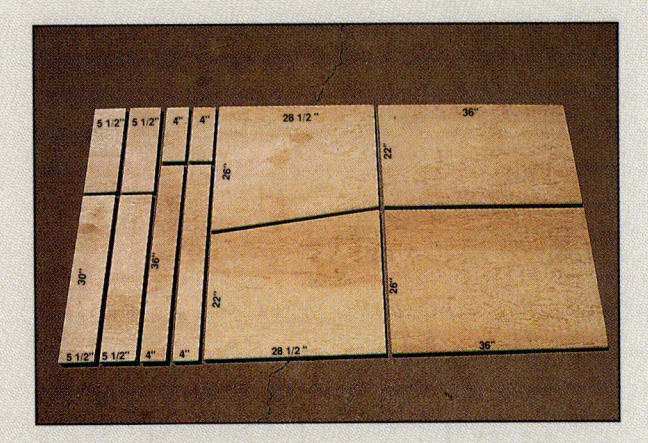

First Carefully cut plywood into pieces of size and shapes shown. Cut 1/2 in. edge slot in 4 x 30 in. pieces for corrugated fiberglass, using table saw blade. Set aside with 4 x 36 in. strips for later use in making cover.

Then Assemble open-bottom coldframe box by fastening with flat-head screws. Drill 1/4 in. pilot holes 1 in. from the end and 1/8 in. from edge in each corner of face and back panel, and every 6 in. along outside edge.

Third Fit fiberglass into slots in 4 x 30 in. pieces and fasten with a round-head screw every 6 in. through top side. Lap each corner with 4 x 36 in. crosspieces, fasten with two flat-head screws. Fasten fiberglass to crosspieces with round-head screws and washers.

Last Attach cover unit to base, fitting hinges 12 in. from each outside corner on inside edge of back and bottom of cover. Cover should fit flat on base when closed. Paint inside flat black with nontoxic exterior latex paint.

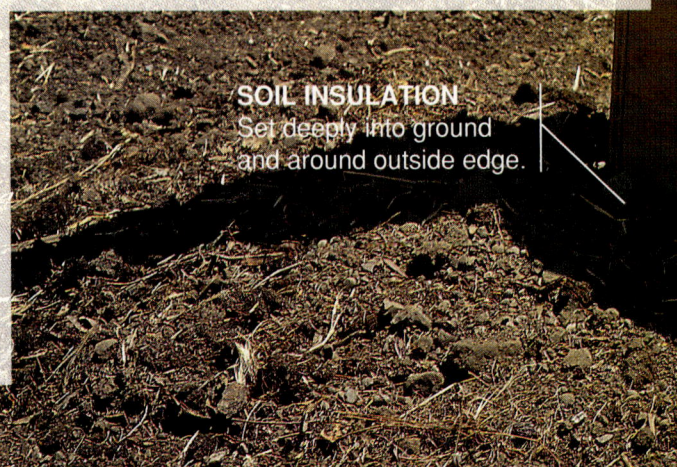

SOIL INSULATION Set deeply into ground and around outside edge.

AIR AND MOISTURE
Allows airflow to prevent overheating and mildew.

EASY ACCESS
Top raises for planting and transplanting.

MATERIALS

1 sheet 3/4 in. ABX plywood

1 26 x 30 in. piece white translucent fiberglass with corrugated ridges in 36 in. direction.

2 2-in. galvanized metal butt hinges, flat-head screws

36 1/4 x 1 1/4 in. flat-head, Phillips-head, brass or galvanized wood screws

18 1/8 x 1/2 in. round-head, Phillips-head brass or galvanized wood screws

18 1/2 x 1/8 in. galvanized washers

PLANTING AND TRANSPLANTING

You can plant most vegetables by following any one of the methods shown here.

Begin After danger of frost, check that morning soil temperature is high enough for seeds to sprout and avoid fungal diseases.

Then Soil should be damp, not dry or sticky. Soil pressed in palm of hand should crumble to loose dirt. Rake planting area smooth and level. Always follow seed packet directions. Plant each seed or transplant using the methods shown.

Furrows and Rows

First Make guide with string stretched between stakes and furrow soil with hoe into rows 4–6 in. high.

Second Press length of hoe handle atop furrow to firm soil to recommended depth. Space seeds along row by gently tapping seed packet.

Third Close sides of row and firm soil around seeds.

Hills and Mounds

First Form hills 6–10 in. high with a trench for later watering. Space mounds as recommended for plant type.

Second Space seeds evenly on top of each hill. Poke each seed into hill to proper depth with finger.

Third Sprinkle loose dirt to cover seeds and press whole hill down firmly with hands to make sure seeds touch soil.

Area Planting

First Turn rake over and smooth planting area. Remove clods and fill any holes.

Second Scatter seeds evenly by hand over entire planting area.

Third Carefully rake seeds into bed to recommended depth. Cover any loose seeds by sprinkling soil over them.

Setting Out Plants

Either Tear away top of peat pots to stop them from wicking water away from plants after planting. Plant whole pot beneath soil surface.

Or Remove plant from plastic or clay pots by tipping upside down into hand. Tap gently to release. Do not pull stem of plant.

Second Plant whole rootball just beneath soil surface (except tomatoes: see pgs. 28–29). Firm ground around plant.

Next Water new plantings by misting gently. Water around transplants. Don't overwater. Keep constantly damp until seeds germinate.

Last Seeds will sprout. If no shoots appear when expected, carefully dig up a few seeds. Replant if not growing.

Extending the Growing Season

Start gardening early, when soil first becomes workable. Soil temperatures rise quickly when covered with sheets of clear or black plastic mulch. Though nighttime temperatures are still frosty, protecting tender transplants started indoors or in a coldframe is easy. Do the same in autumn.

These plants have been hardened and are ready for transplant.

Straw mulch holds ground heat and stops fruit from rotting.

Black plastic warms soil, stops weed growth, holds moisture.

Chips help warm-season plants by preventing nighttime heat loss.

Hot caps, sold in nurseries and garden stores, are easy to use.

Install clear film at planting, then cut when sprouts appear.

Protect rows like hills to limit weed growth and loss of water.

HARDENING TRANSPLANTS

Plants started indoors often suffer when transplanted to cool outdoor weather unless they are "hardened" first.

Harden your tender seedlings by moving them outdoors during the warmer part of the day to a protected location and covering them as it cools at night.

If hard frosts are predicted, move plants back indoors or cover them with a cloth or plastic sheet for protection. Be sure that the cover doesn't touch the plants. This avoids frost and disease damage that begins when water condenses under the cover.

After 4–5 days the plants will have adjusted to the rise and fall of outdoor temperatures and will be much more likely to survive when transplanted to their final bed in the garden.

Plants started outdoors in a coldframe have already partially adjusted to the outdoors. As they near transplant size, open the coldframe during the day, closing it at night. Protect the seedlings from freezing temperatures by closing and covering the coldframe.

Be sure to water transplants thoroughly 24 hours before transplanting to the final location. This necessary step will allow the plants to absorb and store moisture before they undergo the shock of transplanting.

FERTILIZING

Make plants vigorous and more productive by regularly fertilizing during the growing season. Choose fertilizers, using the information on plant nutrients (see pg. 18), then pick from organic, synthetic, liquid, dry and foliar fertilizers, according to your need and purpose.

Dry Fertilizers

First Apply fertilizer 6–8 in. from plant stems.

Then Rake into top inch of soil, water thoroughly. Repeat at intervals shown in Table.

Liquids and Mixed Powders

First Mix or dilute the liquid according to the label.

Then Pour on soil around stems, allow to soak in. Water.

Foliar Fertilizers

First Fill hose-end sprayer, mix as label instructs.

Then Spray onto foliage early so it dries before heat of day.

FERTILIZER APPLICATION

Formula	Oz./Sq. Ft.	Weeks
10-10-10	1/8	4
16-16-16	1/12	6
7-10-10	1/6	6
5-5-0	1/4	4
Manure	1/2	6

Fertilizer Choices and Use

Choose fertilizer according to your needs. Fertilizer may be *balanced* (equal parts of all nutrients) or *complete* (contains all three nutrients); or it may be higher in nitrogen (for foliage development), phosphorus (for vigorous growth), or potassium (for strong roots). Make your choice based on your observations of symptoms and plant development (see pg. 18).

Plants cannot tell synthetic from naturally occurring fertilizers, nor the form that they take. Use one that fits your purpose and plan.

Organic, "natural" fertilizers are made from things like fish, bone, composted manure and minerals, and usually are long lasting. Some may be bulky, smelly or difficult to use or control, but give good results when used as the label instructs.

Synthetic fertilizers are usually made from petroleum or its by-products. They often give quick results, but are concentrated and may burn plants. They must be applied frequently. Following the label is as important as for organic fertilizers.

Fertilizers come in three forms: applied dry, mix dry-into-liquid and liquid. A special category of liquids are *foliar* fertilizers, which are applied to and absorbed by plant leaves and foliage instead of to their roots and the soil.

Vegetables need a steady supply of nutrients each day. Fertilize when planting and every 4–6 weeks all season long. Apply fertilizers as shown in the step-by-step photographs. To prevent burn, always follow the label and water after. If in doubt, apply smaller amounts more often.

Watering

Water, along with nutrients, air and sunlight, is needed for plant growth. For vegetables to have peak flavor and taste, plants should always have just enough water—never too little or too much. Water in the morning hours so plants dry thoroughly and disease spores won't spread.

Overhead Watering

First Use either a hose-end sprayer or sprinkler.

Then Water until a cup placed among the plants is 1–2 in. full.

Root Irrigation

First At planting, create 4-in. furrows for rows and hills.

Then Use a hose-end bubbler to fill each furrow, then move on.

Hand Watering

First Choose a pail or watering can for small or container gardens.

Then Water gently around the plants.

How to Water

When and how to water vegetables is mostly a matter of common sense: Water until the ground has been given a full supply of water that penetrates deeply, whenever needed.

Avoid frequent, shallow watering. Strong roots that resist drying out must grow deep. Just wetting the surface of the soil and then stopping encourages shallow roots that cannot stand a few dry spells.

Don't overwater, particularly if your soil is dense or clay (see pg. 20). When the ground becomes saturated, plants may develop disease or drown because important air cannot reach their roots.

Here's a simple test to see if you should water: Use a trowel or your fingers to dig several inches into the soil, about 8–10 in. from your plants. If the layer of dry soil is more than 3–4 in. thick, it is time to water deeply.

Garden stores and nurseries sell water test meters, with a probe that sticks into the soil to test how much water is present. They are inexpensive and quite accurate.

Water your plants as shown in the step-by-step photographs.

Overhead watering is wasteful but can be used if plants are not yet bearing fruit. Always overhead water in the morning, not in the heat of the day. Allow enough time for any water remaining on the leaves to dry. If evenings are cool, fungus and mold diseases may become a problem (see pg. 62).

It is better to water from beneath, in furrows, by hand or with a drip system.

Give your plants 1–2 in. of water at a time. After soaking in, the ground should be moist at least 6 in. down and should last for 3–4 days unless the weather is hot.

Drip Irrigation

First Easy set-up drip conserves water, supplies single plants.

Then Test running time needed to water each plant on system.

CULTIVATING

Cultivating mixes air into the soil and helps plants receive nutrients while eliminating weed plants that compete with vegetables. Mulching may prevent weeds and help plants last through temperature swings.

Hand Weed Last-resort weeding. Get all roots or some weeds will regrow.

Hoe Uproot small weeds and repair irrigation furrows.

Cultivate Best done when weeds are very young.

Mulch Avoid weeding, hold moisture by mulching with chips, straw or black plastic.

Garden Pests

Insects attack plants above and below ground. Some have rasping mouth parts that chew (beetles, caterpillars and cutworms), others pierce the plant and suck its juices (aphids, mites, whiteflies and leafhoppers) or bore into the plant and eat its flesh (corn earworms, leafminers, and borers). Roots are attacked by maggots, grubs and worms. Many insects go through several different forms in their life cycle: egg, larvae, pupa and adult. In each, they eat or kill plants in one or more of these ways. Prevent infestations (see pgs. 63–65) or use predator insects, hand picking, soaps, naturally occurring insecticides or botanical sprays if an infestation has started. Follow label directions carefully.

Snails and slugs are mollusks that feed at night and on dark days. Again, prevention is the best control. Hand pick in evening or early morning, or use traps or bait if prevention has failed to control them.

CHEWING INSECTS
Thrips, armyworms, beetles, loopers, grasshoppers, moth larvae, caterpillars and hornworms.

PIERCING INSECTS
Aphids, harlequin bugs, leafhoppers, mites and whiteflies.

SNAILS AND SLUGS
Slugs, unlike snails, have no shells. Both eat leaves and stalks of tender plants.

BORING INSECTS
Borers, corn earworms, squash vine borers and corn borers.

SOIL INSECTS
Root maggots, cutworms, flea beetles, nematodes, root weevils and wireworms.

Plant Diseases

MOSAIC VIRUS
Plants must be destroyed. Prevent with resistant strains.

MOLD AND MILDEW
Powdery and downy mildew. Cool, moist conditions favor fungal diseases.

VERTICILLIUM WILT
Soil fungus. Only prevented by using resistant varieties.

DAMPING OFF
Excess moisture and cool soil fungus destroys stem at soil line.

FUSARIUM WILT
Lives in infected soil. Choose disease-resistant varieties.

CLUB ROOT
Roots swell, plant deforms and dies. Keep plantings away from sites where cole crop grew.

PEST AND DISEASE CONTROL

Many organic and chemical controls are sold to reduce or eliminate pests and disease once they become a problem. Avoid the work and cost of using them by stopping pest infestations and diseases before they start.

Healthy garden practices begin at planting. Seed companies offer disease- and pest-resistant strains for most common vegetables. Read labels carefully or ask when buying transplants.

Vigorous plants grown with proper use of fertilizer and good watering practices will resist disease and pests much better than those weakened by poor care. Always water early in the day so that plants dry thoroughly before evening. Molds and mildew grow in cool, damp leaves, stems and soil.

Always pick up dead leaves and other fallen plant matter from the garden. Insects and fungi grow and hide in decaying foliage. Pull up or prune away any infested or diseased plants. Dispose of all clippings and refuse away from the growing area.

If you use disease-control sprays, be sure they are intended for vegetables. Follow all label instructions to the letter. Wash all vegetables thoroughly before eating.

Organic Vegetable Gardening

Look for VFNT letters on seeds, or the words "disease resistant," to prevent common problems.

Healthy plants grown with enough fertilizer and regular watering resist diseases and pests.

Some insects help out in the garden. Ladybird beetles eat aphids and other sucking insects.

Respond correctly and quickly at first sign of insect damage to stop it from spreading.

ORGANIC GARDENING

Many gardeners choose to avoid chemical sprays, powders and fertilizers. Some use sprays derived from naturally occurring sources like chrysanthemums, or use certain insects to control other insects. Others use hand controls—picking, swatting and squashing—or spray their plants with soapy water.

To be effective these methods must be used early and often—at the first sign of insects or disease. Always plant disease- and insect-resistant varieties.

All gardeners should use good, healthy care (see pg. 63) to give plants the best chance to fight off attackers.

Small plots, with many different varieties of vegetables in each, stop large crowds of one-crop insects from growing.

Mulch several times a season to provide insect pests with a convenient hiding place. After a few weeks rake up the mulch and remove it—bugs and all. Put "bug board" paths down your rows. When slugs, snails and insects hide underneath, simply pick up the boards and kill the pests.

Some insects are helpful in your garden—lacewings, trichogramma wasps, praying mantises and ladybird, tiger and ground beetles. Encourage frogs, toads and lizards. Birds help eat insects, snails and slugs, too, but may also eat your crops!

Some damage is unavoidable. Wash surface insects away with mildly soapy water. If infestations cannot be controlled, spray with BT (*Bacillus thuringiensis,* a harmless-to-humans bacteria that kills caterpillars).

Rotenone, ryania and pyrethrum sprays are also safe and effective when used as the label directs.

Making and Using Compost

Adding easy-to-make compost to your garden will help any soil imbalances, since organic compost neutralizes excess acid and alkaline soil. Compost can also be a useful soil amendment, improving texture, aeration and percolation. It also serves as a good mulch material.

MATERIALS

4 x 4 in. posts
2 x 6 in. sideboards
1 x 1 in. slot boards
Posthole cement

Hold raw waste in first section

Turn compost in second and third sections.

Finished, ready-to-use compost.

3-Bin Compost Box

First Assemble construction materials.

Then After digging postholes 18–24 in. deep, set uprights with posthole cement.

Next Fit the horizontal sideboards into the uprights.

Last Use vertical bin spacers to prevent spillage.

USING A COMPOST PILE

Although compost doesn't necessarily add many nutrients of its own, it does loosen native soil and free up its nutrients, and it improves soil texture.

Compost can be made from many organic materials—tree leaves, grass clippings, dead plants, sawdust, kitchen waste, even rotten fruit. Certain materials should be avoided: tree leaves that are highly acid (oak leaves and pine needles) and hay that contains live seeds or sprigs. Anything toxic or diseased should be left out.

Making a compost pile is the simple but time-consuming process of building up layers of organic materials on top of each other, watering the pile and turning it regularly. Natural bacteria and earthworms in the pile soon go to work, heating it up to between 140° and 160°F and decomposing the ingredients into a rich, dark brown substance with the smell of freshly turned humus.

Aeration and watering will ensure that the compost "cooks," but frequent turning will speed up the process. The fastest decomposition occurs with the addition of nitrogen and the use of mechanical turning devices such as drums. A large pile of between 200 and 500 cu. ft. turned every 2 or 3 days will ripen within a few months. Just 1 cu. ft. of compost begins as 4 or 5 cu. ft. of refuse, so build your compost pile to fit your garden size.

Follow these simple instructions to build and use a garden compost pile.

Using Vertical Space

Almost everyone wishes their garden was larger. Enlarge your garden vertically by going upwards for large-space vegetables like melons and squash. Put tomatoes, peppers and eggplants in cages, beans and peas on poles or fences and your cucumber vines on trellises. Light and air circulation is better, so plants tend to be healthier and disease-free. Harvest is easier at eye level too.

Wire Cages

First Cut length of 4–6 in. welded wire mesh 3 1/2 times desired diameter.

Then Use pliers to join into cylinder. Attach to support stake with U-shaped staples.

Last As plant grows weave new shoots back into the cage, leaving flowers outside.

Poles and Twine

First Cut 3 in. diameter pole to final height with 18–24 in. below ground.

Then Install pole at center of 6 ft. diameter circle of 6–8 seedling plants.

Last Put stakes 6 in. outside plant circle. Train new growth up string to pole.

Pea and Bean Fences

First Make enough H-shaped units of 1 x 1 in. sticks for each 18 in. of row.

Then Push H supports into ground 18 in. apart. Plant along center.

Last Tie garden twine between supports. Train plants within twine hedge.

Trellis

First Purchase pre-made trellis or construct from flexible stock.

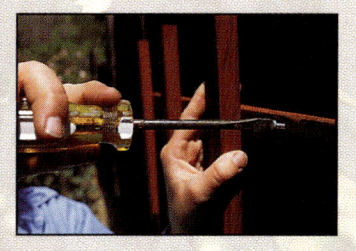

Then Attach to wall or fence with wood screws able to bear weight of plant and fruit.

Last As plant grows support shoots and fruit with stretchable plastic tape.

Harvesting

Harvesting Hints

Planning a season-long harvest is the reward and joy of vegetable gardening. Choose varieties that mature at different times, plant small amounts a few weeks apart, and plant for a planned harvest time. It's more enjoyable to eat a zucchini every other day than to find homes for a basketful.

Each vegetable reaches its peak of flavor and ripeness at a different time. Pick for your intended use—eating raw, cooking fresh, freezing, drying or canning.

Store most root crops right where they grew until frosts threaten. Straw and compost mulches will protect them in the ground.

Pick peas and beans when full and plump if drying is intended, when young and tender for cooking or preserving. Picking all the young pods will extend the crop by developing new flowers; let pods develop fully and flowering will stop.

Cole crops like cabbage will hold on the plant until harvest, but broccoli, brussels sprouts and cauliflower are best picked when buds are young and tender.

Corn—even supersweet varieties—tastes best when picked and used right away, before the sugar in the kernels turns to starch. Peel back the husk and silk, then poke a kernel with your thumbnail. If it is full of sweet juice, pick the ear.

Water leafy greens the evening before harvest, then pick the following morning. The water will make them crisp and more flavorful.

Onions and garlic let you know when they are full grown by starting to develop flowers. Bend their green stalks to the ground, wait 2-4 weeks for final root development, then pull and dry in braids out of the sun.

71

Preserving, Canning, Drying and Freezing

Drying Long shelf life and reduced size and weight makes drying a favorite. Use a dryer or a screened, sunny spot to remove moisture quickly.

Freezing Blanch by boiling, cool in icy water, then drain and quickly freeze to extend the storage life of frozen vegetables.

Canning High-acid and brined vegetables like pickles, tomatoes and sauerkraut can be safely canned using boiling water (212°F).

CAUTION

Botulism Hazard
Not killed by boiling temperatures. Avoid all low-acid, low-salt canning.

STORING AND PRESERVING

The aim of storing and preserving fresh vegetables is to have home-grown taste in your meals after harvest time is over.

Storage—refrigerated, cool and dry, or warm and dry—slows flavor-robbing change in vegetables. As vegetables age, sugars turn into starch. They dry out, lose flavor and become less crisp.

Choose cool, moist storage below 40°F for thin-skinned vegetables with lots of moisture, such as greens or stalks.

Pick cool, dry storage below 50°F for onions and garlic, but a bit more moist for root crops. Allow lots of air to circulate. Don't wash roots, just brush off any clinging soil.

Gourds, winter squash and pumpkins require somewhat warmer, dry storage—up to 60°F. Avoid packing them too tight and allow good air circulation.

Blanching, then freezing, is the choice of most cooks for long-term storage of many vegetables. It preserves flavor, texture and color better than canning. Only use morning-picked vegetables at the peak of their flavor and process them right away.

Drying is another choice for vegetables to be used in stews, soups, casseroles or other moist, slow-cooked dishes. Pick, blanch (if necessary), then dry quickly in a home dryer, available from many retail stores.

Traditional canning and pickling preserves blanched, cooked or partially raw vegetables. After preparation pack vegetables, relishes or sauces into glass jars or metal cans and seal. Heat in a boiling water bath or pressure cooker until all harmful bacteria and spores have been killed. Care must be taken to avoid chance of spoilage or health hazard.

Detailed information and instructions for preserving, canning and freezing may be obtained from your Agricultural Extension Service.

GARDEN TOOLS

Gardening is fun and easy. Having the right tools and materials will save work and time. Large equipment used only rarely should be rented, unless convenience and budget aren't a problem. Here are some basic tools that most vegetable gardeners should have at hand.

Fork

Spade

Pruning shears

Pistol-grip nozzle

Rake

Watering can

Hose-end sprinkler

Cultivating tool

Tiller

Bucket

Trowel

Soaker head

Hoe

Hand spray
applicator bottle

Hose

Hammer

Barrow

Getting Garden Advice

Each state's land grant university has a school or college of agriculture. Any of them can refer you to your local Agricultural Extension Service, available in every county, borough or parish in the United States. Nurseries and garden stores can be easily found in the telephone Yellow Pages. If you have further questions concerning federal or state programs in your area, call the U.S. Department of Agriculture Switchboard at 202-447-USDA.

State University Agricultural Extension Services:

Alabama Auburn University, Auburn, AL 36849 Telephone: (205) 844-4000

Alaska University of Alaska, Fairbanks, AK 99701 Telephone: (904) 474-7211

Arizona University of Arizona, Tucson, AZ 85721 Telephone: (602) 621-2211

Arkansas University of Arkansas, Fayetteville, AR 72701 Telephone: (501) 575-2000

California University of California, Berkeley, CA 94612 Telephone: (415) 987-0040

University of California, Davis, CA 95616 Telephone: (916) 725-0107

University of California, Riverside, CA 92521 Telephone: (714) 787-1012

Colorado University of Colorado, Fort Collins, CO 80523 Telephone: (303) 491-1101

Connecticut University of Connecticut, Storrs, CT 06268 Telephone: (303) 282-7300

Delaware University of Delaware, Newark, DE 19711 Telephone: (302) 735-8200

District of Columbia University of the District of Columbia, Washington, D.C. 20008 Telephone: (202) 282-7300

Florida University of Florida, Gainesville, FL 32611 Telephone: (904) 392-3261

Georgia University of Georgia, Athens, GA 30602 Telephone: (404) 542-3030

Hawaii University of Hawaii, Honolulu, HI 96822 Telephone: (808) 956-8111

Idaho University of Idaho, Moscow, ID 83843 Telephone: (208) 885-6111

Illinois University of Illinois, Urbana, IL 61801 Telephone: (217) 333-1000

Indiana Purdue University, Lafayette, IN 47901 Telephone: (317) 494-4600

Iowa Iowa State University, Ames, IA 50010 Telephone: (515) 294-4111

Kansas Kansas State University, Manhattan, KS 66506 Telephone: (913) 532-6011

Kentucky University of Kentucky, Lexington, KY 40506 Telephone: (606) 257-9000

Louisiana Louisiana State University, Baton Rouge, LA 70893 Telephone: (504) 388-3202

Maine University of Maine, Orono, ME 04469 Telephone: (207) 581-1110

Maryland University of Maryland, College Park, MD 20742 Telephone: (301) 454-0100

Massachusetts University of Massachusetts, Amherst, MA 01003 Telephone: (413) 545-0111

Michigan Michigan State University, East Lansing, MI 48824 Telephone: (517) 355-1855

Minnesota University of Minnesota, St. Paul, MN 55101 Telephone: (612) 325-2131

Mississippi Mississippi State University, MS 39762 Telephone: (601) 325-2131

Missouri University of Missouri, Columbia, MO 65201 Telephone: (314) 882-2121

Montana Montana State University, Bozeman, MT 59715 Telephone: (406) 994-0211

Nebraska University of Nebraska, Lincoln, NE 68503 Telephone: (402) 472-7211

Nevada University of Nevada-Reno, Reno, NV 89507 Telephone: (702) 784-6611

New Hampshire University of New Hampshire, Durham, NH 03824 Telephone: (603) 862-1234

New Jersey Rutgers University, New Brunswick, NJ 08903 Telephone: (201) 932-1766

New Mexico New Mexico State University, Las Cruces, NM 88003 Telephone: (505) 646-0111

New York Cornell University, Ithaca, NY 14850 Telephone: (607) 256-1000

North Carolina Duke University, Durham, NC 27706 Telephone: (919) 684-2135

North Dakota North Dakota State University, Fargo, ND 58105 Telephone: (702) 237-9011

Ohio Ohio State University, Columbus, OH 43210 Telephone: (614) 422-6446

Oklahoma Oklahoma State University, Stillwater, OK 74708 Telephone: (405) 744-5000

Oregon Oregon State University, Corvallis, OR 97331 Telephone: (503) 754-0123

Pennsylvania Pennsylvania State University, University Park, PA 16802 Telephone: (814) 865-4700

Puerto Rico University of Puerto Rico, Mayaguez, PR 00708 Telephone: (809) 832-4040

Rhode Island University of Rhode Island, Kingston, RI 02881 Telephone: (401) 792-1000

South Carolina Clemson University, Clemson, SC 29634 Telephone: (803) 656-3311

South Dakota South Dakota State University, Brookings, SD 57007 Telephone: (605) 688-4151

Tennessee University of Tennessee, Knoxville, TN 37901 Telephone: (615) 974-0111

Texas Texas A & M University, College Station, TX 77843 Telephone: (409) 845-4747

Texas Technological University, Lubbock, TX 79409 Telephone: (806) 742-2808

Utah Utah State University, Logan, UT 84321 Telephone: (801) 750-1000

Vermont University of Vermont, Burlington, VT 05401 Telephone: (802) 656-3131

Virginia Virginia Polytechnic Institute, Blacksburg, VA 24061 Telephone: (703) 231-6000

Washington Washington State University, Pullman, WA 99164 Telephone: (509) 335-3564

West Virginia University of West Virginia, Morgantown, WV 26506 Telephone: (304) 293-0111

Wisconsin University of Wisconsin, Madison, WI 53706 Telephone: (608) 262-1234

Wyoming University of Wyoming, Laramie, WY 82070 Telephone: (307) 766-4133

HELP AND INFORMATION

Most of the information you will need to grow a successful vegetable garden is contained in these pages. Vegetable gardening is a common-sense pastime, and refreshing your memory by looking at the step-by-step pictures for each project will help guide you through it.

Local gardening experts exist everywhere. Many local radio stations broadcast weekly programs with garden tips suited to your climate, region and soil. Newspapers and television programs provide more general information about gardening.

Part of the fun of gardening is meeting other gardeners and sharing your triumphs and failures. When you see a fellow vegetable gardener with a beautiful plot, stop by and ask what techniques he or she has found work best in your area. Most will be happy to put down their hoe and chat—bragging and giving advice is as much fun for gardeners as it is for those who catch fish!

When more expert advice is needed, visit your local nursery or garden store. These professional gardeners want your gardening experience to be a success because it's good business. Ask for their help and suggestions. They usually have a library of reference books, know local growers and wholesale nurseries and have heard what works and what doesn't.

Most expert of all are instructors and assistants at the U.S. Department of Agriculture Extension offices and at agricultural universities. Many are listed here.

As you build up your storehouse of knowledge about gardening you'll become an expert, too!

INDEX

A
acidic soil, 18
advice, professional gardening, 76–77
Agricultural Extension Service, 19, 73
  listed by state, 76–77
alkaline soil, 18
amaranth, 31
amendment
  compost, 66–67
  organic, 21
aphids, 61
applied dry fertilizers, 54–55
area planting, method of, 51
armyworms, 61
artichokes, 44
asparagus, 45
asparagus beans, 38
asparagus cowpeas, 39

B
Bacillus thuringiensis, 65
balanced fertilizers
  choosing, 55
  defined, 19
basil, 46
beans
  varieties listed, 39
  growing, 38–39
  harvesting, 70
beetles, 61
beets, cooking uses, 34
black plastic, protecting with, 52
blanching vegetables, advantages of, 73
blood meal, 18
bone meal, 18
borers, 61
boring insects, types listed, 61
broccoli, harvesting, 33, 70
brussels sprouts, harvesting, 32, 70
bush beans, varieties listed, 39
bush plants, growing, 39

C
cabbage
  harvesting, 70
  types listed, 33
canning vegetables, 72–73
cantaloupes, types listed, 36
caraway, 46
carrots, varieties, 34
caterpillars, 61
catnip, 46
cauliflower
  growing, 33
  harvesting, 70
chemical sprays
  avoiding, 65
  using, 63
chervil, 46
chewing insects, types listed, 61
chicory, 31
Chinese cabbage, cooking uses, 32
Chinese parsley, 44–47. *See also* coriander
chives, 46
choosing garden vegetables, 24–25
chop suey greens, 31
chrysanthemums edible, 31
cilantro, 47. *See also* coriander
clay soil, 20–21
climate, vegetables and, 9
club root, described, 62
cocozelle (marrow) squash, 37
coldframe
  building a, 48–49
  protecting from freeze in, 52–53
  transplanting in a, 53
cole vegetables
  harvesting, 70
  listed, 32–33
collards, 32
complete fertilizers
  choosing, 55
  defined, 19
compost
  building a bin, 67
  making and using, 66–67
  using a pile, 67
composted manure
  adding, 21
  organic fertilizer, 18
cool-season vegetables
  advantages of, 9
  choosing, 24–25
coles as, 32–33
coriander, 47
corn
  harvesting, 70
  pests, 61
  types listed, 42–43
corn borers, 61
corn earworm, 61
Costoluto tomatoes, 29
cottonseed meal, 18
cress, 31
crowns, planting, 45
cucumbers, types listed, 36
cultivating
  benefits and methods of, 58–59
  tool, 74
cutworms, 61

D
damage
  avoiding plant, 52–53
  hand control of, 65
  insect, 65
damping off, described, 62
determinate plants, defined, 29
dill, 46
disease, control, 62–63
disease-control sprays, using, 63
disease damage, avoiding, 52–53
diseases
  avoiding, 65
  plant, 62–63
drip irrigation, 57
dry fertilizers, 54
drying vegetables, 72–73

E
earthworms, compost and, 67
eggplants
  Japanese, 40
  serving, 40
equipment, 74

F
fences, using, 69
fennel, 47
fertilizer burn, avoiding, 55
fertilizers
  application of, 54
  avoiding burn, 19, 55
  balanced, 19
  choosing and using, 19, 55
  complete, 19
  organic, 18
  synthetic, 19
  types of, 54
fish emulsion, 18
fish meal, 18
flea beetles, 61
foliage development, 55
foliar fertilizers, 54–55
freezing vegetables, 72–73
frogs, as beneficial, 65
frost damage, avoiding, 52–53
full season vegetables, 24
fungus diseases, avoiding, 57
furrows
  planting method, 50
  watering in, 57
fusarium wilt
  described, 63
  resistance to, 29

G
garden
  compost pile, 67
  determining space for, 13
  eliminating weeds, 58–59
  enlarging, 68–69
  extending season, 52–53
  five types of, 14–15
  good soil, 20–21
  necessary nutrients, 18–19
  organic vegetable, 64–65
  pest and disease control, 62–63
  pests, 60–61
  planning, 16–17
  planning water supply, 16–17
  preparing soil, 16–18
  professional advice for, 76–77
  selecting site for, 12–13
  sprays used in, 65
  tools listed for, 74–75
  using vertical space in, 68–69
  watering, 56–57
garlic
  harvesting, 70
  root vegetable, 35
  storing, 73
gourds
  storing, 73
  types listed, 37
granite, pulverized, 19
grasshoppers, 61
greens, harvesting, 70

H
ground bark, adding, 21
ground beetles, as beneficial, 65
growing season
  determining, 20–11
  extending, 52–53
growth
  phosphorus and, 18
  stunted, 19
  vigorous, 55

hand controls, for plant damage, 65
hand watering, 56
hand weeding, 58
hardening transplants, 53
harlequin bugs, 61
harvesting, hints for, 70
help, agencies providing, 76–77
herbs, growing, 46–47
hills, planting method for, 50
hoe, 58
honeydews, 36
hoof-and-horn meal, 18
hornworms, 61
hot caps, using, 53
humus, 20, 67

I
indeterminate plants, defined, 29
information, agencies providing, 76–77
insects
  beneficial, 65
  life cycle of, 60

K
kale, cooking uses, 32
kohlrabi, cooking, 33

L
lacewings, as beneficial, 65
ladybird beetles, as beneficial, 65
leafhoppers, 61
leafy greens
  harvesting, 70
  types listed, 30–31
leaves, nitrogen and, 18
leeks, cooking uses, 35
lettuce, types listed, 30
liquid fertilizers, 54–55
lizards, as beneficial, 65
loam, 20–21
loopers, 61
luffa-sponge gourds, 37

M
manure, composted, 18
melons, types listed, 36
mildew, described, 62
mites, 61
mix dry-into-liquid fertilizers, 54–55
mixed greens, listed, 31
mold diseases
  avoiding, 57
  described, 62
mosaic virus, described, 62
moth larvae, 61

78

mounds, planting method for, 50
mulch
  compost as, 66
  organic gardening, 65
  protecting with, 52
  for weed control, 59
mustards, cooking uses, 31

N
nature, working with, 8-9
nematodes
  compost and, 67
  as garden pest, 61
  resistance to, 29
nitrogen, for foliage development, 18, 55
NK Law & Garden Co., 80
N P K code, 19
nutrients
  cultivating and, 58
  necessary garden, 18-19
  needed, 55

O
okra, growing, 38-39
onions
  cooking uses, 35
  harvesting, 70
  storing, 73
oregano, 47
organic amendments, listed, 21
organic fertilizers, 54-55
  listed, 18
organic vegetable gardening, 64-65
overhead watering, 56-57
overwatering, dangers of, 57

P
parsley, 35, 46
parsnip, 35
peas
  growing, 38-39
  harvesting, 70
  varieties listed, 39
peat moss, adding, 21
peppermint, 47
peppers
  chili, 40
  serving, 40
  sweet types listed, 41
perennial vegetables
  growing, 44-45
  planting, 45
pests
  avoiding, 65
  controlling, 62-63
  garden, 60-61
  life cycle of, 60
phosphoric acid, 19
phosphorus, need for, 18, 55
piercing insects, types listed, 61
plant beds
  building raised, 22-23
  pest and disease control, 62-63
  planning, 16-17
plant diseases, types listed, 62-63
planting

determining date for, 10-11
  methods of, 50-51
  preparing for, 18-19
plants
  determinate, 29
  indeterminate, 29
  pole varieties vs. bush, 39
  protecting from freeze, 52-53
  vine types listed, 36-37
  watering, 56-57
pole beans, varieties listed, 39
poles, using, 69
pole snap beans, 38
pole variety plants, growing, 39
popcorn, harvesting, 42
potash, 18-19
potassium, need for, 18, 55
potatoes, types listed, 35
praying mantises, as beneficial, 65
preserving vegetables, 24, 72-73
pumpkins
  storing, 73
  types listed, 37
pyrethrum sprays, 65

R
radishes, varieties, 34
raised-bed planters, building, 22-23
rhizomes, planting, 45
rhubarb, 44
root crops, harvesting, 70
root irrigation, 56
root maggots, 61
roots
  development, 55
  potassium and, 18
root vegetables, listed, 34-35
root weevils, 61
roquette, cooking uses, 31
rosemary, 47
rotenone sprays, 65
rows, planting method, 50
rutabaga, cooking uses, 35
ryania sprays, 65

S
sage, 47
salad vegetables, 24
salsify, 35
sandy soil, 20-21
sawdust, adding, 21
scallop squash, 37
scarlet runner beans, 38
season
  extending growing, 52-53
  growing, 10-11
seasonings, growing, 46-47
seedlings, hardening, 53
seeds, disease resistant, 65
setting out plants, planting method, 51
shallots, cooking uses, 35
silt, 20
slugs, 60
snails, 60
soil
  amendments, 66-67
  correcting imbalance, 66-67
  defining good, 20-21
  during planting, 50
  during transplanting, 50
  ideal, 21
  insects listed, 61
  preparing, 16-18
sorrel, 45, 47
soybeans, 38
specialty beans, types listed, 38
spinach, planting, 30
spoilage, avoiding, 72-73
sprays
  used in organic gardening, 65
  using disease-control, 63
squash
  storing, 73
  summer types, 37
  winter types, 37
squash vine borers, 61
State University Services, listed, 76-77
summer savory, 46
summer squash, types listed, 37
sunflowers, growing, 44
superphosphate, 19
sweet corn, types listed, 43
sweet marjoram, 47
sweet peppers, types listed, 41
sweet potatoes, types listed, 35
swiss chard, cooking uses, 31
synthetic fertilizers
  described, 54-55
  listed, 19

T
table vegetables, 24
tarragon, 47
thrips, 61
thyme, 47
toads, as beneficial, 65
tobacco mosaic virus, resistance to, 29
tomatillo, 45
tomatoes
  cape gooseberry, 45
  disease-resistance varieties, 29
  ground cherry, 45
  growing, 28-29
  growing from seedlings, 29
  strawberry, 45
  types listed, 28-29
tools, garden, 74-75
transplanting
  hardening plants for, 52-53
  methods of, 50-51
  watering and, 53
trellis, using, 69
trichogram, as beneficial, 65
turnip
  cooking uses, 35
  greens, 31
twine, using, 69

U
USDA growing zone number, 10-11
U.S. Department of Agriculture Switchboard, number for, 76

V
vegetables
  blanching, 73
  canning, 72-73
  choosing garden, 24-25
  cole, 32-33
  cool-season, 9
  drying, 72-73
  freezing, 72-73
  full season, 25
  leafy green, 30-31, 70
  nutrients needed, 55
  organic gardening, 64-65
  perennial, 44-45
  preserving, 24, 72-73
  root, 34-35
  salad, 24
  table, 24
  warm-season, 9
vertical space, using garden, 68-69
verticillium wilt
  described, 62
  resistance to, 29
VFNT letters, 65
vine plants, types listed, 36-37

W
warm-season vegetables, 9
  choosing, 24-25
  coldframe for, 48-49
wasps, as beneficial, 65
watering
  during planting, 51
  during transplanting, 51, 53
  how to, 57
  methods of, 56-57
  planning, 16-17
  to resist pest and disease, 63
watermelons, 36
water test meters, using, 57
weeds, eliminating, 58-59.
  See also cultivating
whiteflies, 61
white potatoes, 35
winter savory, 47
winter squash, 37
  storing, 73
wire cages, using, 68
wireworms, 61
wood ashes, 18-19

Y
yellowing, plant, 19

79

A Note From NK Lawn and Garden Co.

For more than 100 years, since its founding in Minneapolis, Minnesota, NK Lawn & Garden has provided gardeners with the finest quality seed and other garden products.

We doubt that our leaders, Jesse E. Northrup and Preston King, would recognize their seed company today, but gardeners everywhere in the U.S. still rely on NK Lawn & Garden's knowledge and experience at planting time.

We are pleased to be able to share this practical experience with you through this ongoing series of easy-to-use gardening books.

Here you'll find hundreds of years of gardening experience distilled into easy-to-understand text and step-by-step pictures. Every popular gardening subject is included.

As you use the information in these books, we hope you'll also try our lawn and garden products. They're available at your local garden retailer.

There's nothing more satisfying than a successful, beautiful garden. There's something special about the color of blooming flowers and the flavor of home-grown garden vegetables.

We understand how special you feel about growing things—and NK Lawn & Garden feels the same way, too. After all, we've been a friend to gardeners everywhere since 1884.